HUGE LESSONS LEARNED

In the

TRENCHES of LIFE

Business Executives as well as Homeowners face more than a few challenges in life which are awesome teachers to protect your future.

Get the free Internet Marketing series from respected Trainers that we know like and Trust at DonMonteith.com

Why I wrote this book...

The primary reason for writing this book is an attempt to alert you to things that can happen in your future world of business and unexpected family issues.

Frankly, I have a hard time believing how easily each of us can be "hoodwinked" (sucker punched!) by business partners, close family members, siblings, and even cousins we hardly know.

Hopefully, you'll miss most of these things but for some reason it raises its ugly head when least expected and the experience is mind boggling to say the least.

You'll never have the same experiences we did but there are plenty more just waiting for you on the path called life, in the trenches.

"Everyone has a story to tell" and learning from our experiences may help you to miss them in your future, that's our goal.

Should YOU read this book?

Maybe you don't need to learn anything from us. Don't know about that, but we need to share the <u>lessons</u> <u>learned</u> anyway, "just in case."

Why? It's mainly because we don't want any of the bad ones repeated in your lifetime, especially the ones that can cost you money or give off bad vibes in your career or cause family distress.

Experience is <u>good</u> and often a <u>great</u> <u>teacher</u>, but it can turn into expensive <u>lessons</u> <u>learned</u> if you have to earn and learn everything on your own.

Truth is.... our hope is that 97% of the things we share with you are awesome, great or good things to know about your business and your future success in life.

INTRODUCTION

After a 35 year career building offline businesses, several were franchised services and our largest multi-million dollar business began as a franchise, too.

Unfortunately, our very first franchisor went bankrupt and we ended up joining a big national firm in the same service business.

However, it gets worse before it gets better. The national firm was a <u>household name</u> that you'd recognize immediately but the name of the firm is not important. It's the change in leadership that made the difference.

It was simply the
GREED of top management in our particular
division that cost them everything, the entire
division simply disappeared in the end.

As a Regional Manager with six (6) branches,
four (4) built from the ground up, we had
turned those assets into valuable cash cows
for the division.

Unfortunately for the firm, one of their top
executives decided he could make a name for
himself off the backs of the Regional
Managers.

You can see it coming, right? Get rid of all
those high salaries by simply downsizing (fire
all the Regional Managers) then slide the

extra cash to the bottom line. Can you see him "drooling" over his huge bonus coming down the pike into his personal account?

Fortunately for us, the greedy "executive" got his due and lost the whole ship to some of the Regional Managers who ended up with the business under their own umbrella.

Every Sunday we say this powerful Mantra in church.... "God is GOOD all the time" and "All the time God is GOOD!

TABLE OF CONTENTS

YOUR FIRST DAY

We can "assume" many things but will probably be wrong 99% of the time trying to connect with everyone reading this book.

Some of you are likely "old-timers" and been in business for many years and made all the mistakes, like we did, on your own. Others of you are newbies but want to get ahead of the curve as new entrepreneurs.

We write very fast so hang with us and see what you can learn in the shortest time frame. Before long, you'll be at the very end of this chapter.

Grab your pen and paper so you can write down every

idea that surfaces or discover a new opportunity that can help you excel in your daily life.

There are no real surprises when you "read" about our experiences rather than "walk the walk" in person where you'll feel every pain, punch and kick just like we did in the trenches.

However, old or new, none of us will ever "know it all". We're very confident that some of the challenges and lessons learned will never cross your path, but we do believe that some of the lessons learned will be a direct hit and the escape hatch is open to save your business, your life, even your inheritance.

Nothing beats living life with GRATITUDE followed up with thanksgiving for all things. Some of the most interesting experiences we want to share with you seemed very bad until hindsight (review) revealed the other side for us and turned it into a good thing.

It's been suggested that everyone (including you) has a "story to tell" and share with the world. At this juncture of life and time for us, it seems the right thing to do.

IF we help ONE entrepreneur, a homeowner or simply one individual learn how to avoid a bad experience or earn millions because of shared experiences we are glad that we took the time to write this book.

Some of the lessons learned were in Business College, but most of them were learned in the <u>trenches</u> on a daily basis where we like to say, "Life happens, keep the faith."

Many lessons were learned in the SHK [School of Hard knocks!] where the "rubber meets the road" on our way to success through the trenches, where we live and learn.

Maybe 15 <u>Lessons</u> <u>Learned</u> is more than enough for those who are willing to listen.

I can already hear some folks (maybe you!) saying "that would never happen" or a few spouting obscene words like stupid, dumb, or idiot for starters. I certainly understand and often agree with you.

Problems do seem to show up when least expected. There are many entrepreneurs who have a high risk mentality, taking chances at inopportune times, dumb junctures or at very interesting venues.

What I do know.... had we known some of the lessons learned prior to experiencing them, we'd be much wealthier or as some would say, filthy rich, rather than just "happily" rich in all things good.

Knowing is preferred rather than failing to take heed before disaster strikes. No one reading this book will experience all of the challenges we have, however, there are hundreds, probably thousands, more to choose from along your life's path.

Every business executive, every homeowner, married, single or otherwise faces a never ending stream of challenges and experiences to face each day of your life.

You'll never hear about Lessons Learned from your friends at the club, your golf buddies, or in your church family. In most cases, people don't like to talk about their mistakes or errors in judgment or loss.

Usually, it's very embarrassing to us and not something you want to share with your competitors, even friends, in the marketplace.

At least for us, we NEVER talk about anything outside of our company walls for self-protection or simple fear.

Our experiences in the business, especially financial, profit and loss, our latest equipment purchases, savings, special deals, employees, ownership is private and kept within the confines of the executive offices.

Why would anyone do otherwise? First, bad news travels faster than lightning into your competitors' gossip mill, grapevine.

Suddenly, you're hearing rumors that your bills are not being paid on time or you've fired 1/2 your staff and just maybe you're heading for bankruptcy rather than fine tuning your business.

Unfortunately, these fear of failure rumors, true or not, are dealt with as truth and reality. Your employees begin to talk, ask a few questions, begin to look for other jobs out of some fear that's been caused by unsupported rumors.

Companies reduce staff for many reasons, maybe a change in your future direction, you've added new systems, new equipment or turned to automation to help cut cost and reduce or replace staff.

Maybe you've hired a new employee or two from your local competitors or you've begun recruiting a few graduates from area colleges.

All actions are recognized as SOP [Standard Operating Procedure] for your business.

New and seasoned business owners have to recognize that there will always be something to worry about, maybe it snows 3 feet deep and no one shows up for work or you're on a Caribbean Cruise or basking in the Maui sunshine while you're on vacation with your family. You deserve it, just do it!

Yes, there really are 15 Lessons Learned to share with you but the real challenge is writing them down, explaining each one with clarity so any misunderstanding is minimized to the bare facts.

Most of the Lessons Learned are business related but a few reach back to my childhood, my family and my Dad's own business experiences. Many things we can learn simply watching and listening to others.

Truth is, it may not grab your gut like it does mine, even today, but I'll share with you a few tidbits of very early exposure to insider talk standing around the old potbelly stove in the warehouse office.

Like most teenagers, I didn't want to work at Dad's office, from the very beginning, I didn't like it. Yes, I did work there a few months and then moved on to a bank job the day I turned 16 years old. No, they didn't call me Mr. President but being the "mail boy" was almost as good.

One lesson I did learn from Mr. President at the time, at least it was reported back to me, that he had bought a new Ford Convertible from the local dealer, it was a beauty, black with red leather interior, and he insisted (made sure) the salesman earned a full ten percent (10%) commission, more like 25% today.

Anyhow, I was very impressed by his concern about the salesman's welfare and income. Big deal? You decide. I thought it was and still do.

Was that an influence "long-term" in my life? Did it plant a seed that influences my "tipping" attitude and concern for those who wait on us in restaurants and other places where service is important?

Actually, that was a big Lesson Learned but it slipped in as a freebie so let's hope the next 15 will come with similar or greater value.

The 15 Lessons Learned

LESSON LEARNED #1 - Never join a business associate or franchisor without doing your due diligence or vetting the owner.

Reality is you're investing your money, your time and your energy.

Joining forces with anyone or any enterprise outside your value system seldom turns into your best decision as a future business owner.

Sidebar: Life decisions, too! Marriage, divorce, dating, etc. all require your best wisdom.

Most of the time we're looking backwards into our past AFTER realizing that our decisions were made for the wrong reasons.

Never rush into anything is good advice most of the time in all circumstances. Few things require an immediate decision from us.

My First Business Decision

In my early life the mail order business intrigued (grabbed) my interest. One thing stands out above all else about the association owner, basically a franchisor.

Yes, I spent four (4) years along with fifty (50) associates (franchisees) that lived across the USA. Most were older, more experienced in the business arena.

Tom (the owner) was 32 years old and I was 21 just out of Business College. He was smart, articulate and later proved himself to be a "Slick Willie" business owner, to our regret.

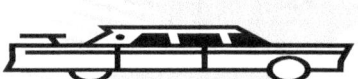

Upon arrival at the airport, Tom picked me up in his beautiful new white Cadillac and drove us over to his newly furnished private villa for potential associates. His sidekick (Jim) was riding "shotgun" which seemed OK.

Nothing appeared to be out of line and the very next morning he (or Jim) picked me up and we drove over to a very attractive, well-furnished business office and warehouse. It was obvious that Tom was in full control and business was great (it appeared).

My mind still reels from his conversation overheard on the phone that morning. I was outside his office when he hollered out "who is on that GD phone" which should have brought an immediate alert to my own conscience as a Christian but I let it slide.

Yes, I did join as an associate (franchisee) and invested funds into his mail-order business to sell merchandise across America through the US Postal Service.

In summary, we had a very good business experience because Tom was a genius copywriter, he negotiated excellent contracts with vendors on behalf of the associates which allowed each of us to make a good profit as business owners.

After 4.5 years, Tom suddenly disappeared and all associates ended up out of business within a couple of months.

Obviously, hindsight tells us there was a verbal alert that we should have listened to in the beginning, on the first day, but the excitement of owning a business won out.

I hear you loud and clear, we had the same questions. Where did he go or "why" was more important to us. Speculation came from all around but not one, not even Jim (his sidekick), would know for sure.

Did Tom have a marital problem? Was the IRS on his tail? Did a vendor get cheated in a new business deal? All we knew back then and now, Tom showed up in Hong Kong without a word back to the Associates.

<u>Lesson</u> <u>Learned</u>: #2 – There are NO guarantees in any business. It would be nice if there were somebody hanging out in the back office with a stun gun or a big bat on the ready. Not a good idea but it really felt like a super idea for the moment.

OK, I'm with you on this one. IF you screw up, sign your name on the contract it means if things don't work out, suck it up!

Sidebar – You'll think I'm a big city lawyer or some legal counsel extraordinary seeking a new client but nothing is further from the truth.

I simply learned what it means to document every agreement in detail for peace of mind and I encourage you to do the same for your own benefit and preservation of your assets.

<u>Lesson</u> <u>Learned</u> #3 - Never sign any agreement or contract that you don't understand. Your <u>own</u> legal counsel is mandatory and without exception any time you're into a negotiation.

Everyone (including YOU!) is entitled to seek out their very best benefits and rewards for themselves along with all parties negotiating the end results of an agreement.

You may be buying a franchise or maybe you and a good friend, an old college roommate or just an old buddy from the neighborhood, are talking about going into business together.

Carefully weigh your contribution to the total package or expect to be shortchanged in the deal. You have to spell out everything, word for word, with legal counsel on YOUR team.

It may seem like "no big deal" in the beginning but hopefully you'll be a huge success in your own business career and know that the BIG bucks change hands when you eventually sell out and retire.

A New Partnership

Looking back on our first business day in a new partnership venture makes me mad and disappointed at the same time. An obvious lesson learned from (hindsight) is to ALWAYS have <u>your</u> <u>own</u> <u>legal</u> <u>counsel</u>, probably your accountant, too, to make sure the agreement is a win/win or unfortunately you can end up with a contract/agreement outside or less than you expected as a new business partner.

When you receive STOCK ownership in a business be aware that some impactful things can happen in your future that you don't expect but there are a few legal ways to protect your piece of the business.

Assume that you have a new partner, maybe 2 or 3, that decide to do something <u>outside</u> the parameters of your agreement but failed to include you in the "loop."

In the beginning it seems a non-issue until it actually happens to you and your business. Sometime in the future, maybe 10+ years later, you suddenly get a surprise call from your banker and his message almost causes you to have a cardiac arrest.

Your trusted Banker (he gives you an inside scoop) calls your office looking for one of your partners. Actually, the "scoop" is two or three years late but now you know. One of your trusted partners has used her stock certificate/s to borrow money to buy another business.

"She" knew that using her stock certificate as a <u>guarantee document</u> to borrow money was

<u>NOT</u> <u>allowed</u> and was documented (written into) the original stock owners' agreement.

Unfortunately, a special notice should have been written across (the front) of each stockholders certificate on day ONE but the excitement of the day pushed it to the back burner to be forgotten.

Where's the problem? Exactly, NO ONE "bothered" to take a pen and post the notice on each certificate. HER banker (yours too!) would have been alerted to the simple stock protection notice for "all to see".

Why has this now turned into YOUR problem? IF your partners-owners now owe the bank repayment of her loan, interest and probably late fees the bank is looking for "wholeness" and you could end up with a new partner named First United Bank of (your town!)

Hindsight tells us there should be a "what if" inside your original stock owners' agreement (a little legalese) to protect the certificate holders when bad "Karma" slips into the ranks and someone tries to pull a fast one on the side. Obviously, she "thought" no one would ever know, imagine that from a trusted partner.

In summary, rather than beat a dead horse, your current stock values along with all the owners may be at risk. Hopefully, your stock value has gone up over the years in business or worthless is a possibility depending on the size of "her" debt with the bank.

Your bigger question is, how much is the company stock worth today? Depending on circumstances, it may prove to be a good decision for the firm to pay off the partner's debt to the bank and let her repay your company or in some cases to give up her stock and leave her employment behind.

Another possibility is that the bank can sell her stock to the highest bidder and remove it from their portfolio or just maybe you're about to get a new partnership with the bank or an <u>unknown</u> <u>buyer</u>.

Just know that this scene is reason to have your own legal counsel for protection of your assets from day one, <u>not</u> later. I'm not making this stuff up sitting here on the couch. My brain doesn't even begin to come up with some of the "stuff" faced as a business owner.

I've known partners in business who jumped in "bed" with a competitor at the first sign of a business slowdown, screw the others, let the chips fall but not on this guy with a loyalty fungus. It happens!!

By now, you're beginning to think that we're saying everyone is greedy and self-serving.

Not necessarily true, however, it's difficult to know "who is and who isn't" so it's best to treat everyone the same.

<u>Lesson</u> <u>Learned</u> #4 – Don't overlook simple coding on your stock certificates, like "Cannot be used to borrow funds" or "not to be used for personal gain" with any person or financial institution. Be sure every certificate has been coded by your legal advisors.

This "to do" lesson is so simple even a 3rd grader would know NOT to leave it up to the office clerk but it happens, nobody did it.

All your hard work to build the business, protect the family jewels, yet this simple failure can put your entire portfolio in jeopardy. A long explanation is a time waster but driving the point home is worth it.

Too many of us are clueless about how quickly a business can be forced out of business without recourse.

We won't even mention what happens if you get in the crosshairs of the IRS by not paying your taxes. IF you're out of cash, close the doors of your business today.

<u>Lesson</u> <u>Learned</u> #5 – Recruit and pay top salaries, bonuses and perks for the best employees, hire highly rated professionals with exceptional credentials to work in or on your business.

Usually, a disaster is waiting when you hire friends or family members. (There are exceptions but understand that it comes with high risk)

Sidebar: Right up front, I have to tell you that we hired family in our business and it worked out well for us. We were very fortunate but still think your awareness is important because jealousies or favoritism can rattle the very core of your business and employees.

Sometimes our corporate policies are flawed in the hiring process and most of us can attest to good and bad practices as well as experiences we'd rather miss.

People (employees) selection to run your business is probably your most important decision. Few things have a greater impact on your own business bottom line (profits) than the knowledge of your business partner/s and the expertise of your employees, the good ones will PAY for themselves.

Every one of us, YOU, your business partners, your employees all carry some of their own "baggage", NO exceptions. It may be an attitude or behavioral issues, lack of interest, no motivation and other things you know that can and will impact your business success.

There's always the question about family, siblings, children of partners, too. Is it a good business practice to hire family members?

My answer is maybe, maybe not could be the better answer. Sometimes jealousies surface within the staff or between siblings that can cause unrest in the ranks.

Qualifications, talent, skills, knowledge of the business itself are your better choices to build a successful business in the shortest time period.

Should you bring in a business partner to share ownership of the business? Lots of good reasons come to mind.

Maybe you can build your business much faster with exceptional expertise on the team, financial resources, valuable experiences in the marketplace, plus the "right" connections are just a few values worth considering.

Your biggest decision is to know the "WHY" then set up your business with expertise and guidance along with a win/win structure for fairness and long-term success.

With that said, particularly for low cost business models, there are good reasons to hold on to 100% company ownership. Same goes for your personal decisions, too.

The decision making process changes with less than 51% stock ownership while anyone with 49% or less has NO authority making power except that which is given or allowed by the majority owner.

In the course of my business career there have been many times that simply listening to some innocent talk around the water cooler or the light pole proved very valuable.

One sunny day an Electrician was working on the outside lamp post at our home. Names slip out of his mouth, a non-suspecting person just making small talk.

Innocently, the electrician mentioned a name which we suddenly recognized as the name of a partner's girlfriend and her sister. He had recently done some electrical work at her apartment, too. It turns out that the sister had been secretly hired by the partner without the knowledge of the other partners which should have never happened.

It's amazing how an innocent comment can reveal the names of people that you'd never suspect as closely connected. Not always the discovery of bad "karma" in your company. It may turn into you hiring a new employee or discovering a business link to a million dollar account, a little wishful thinking, but it does happen.

Relationships are your primary keys to the next valuable employee, an awesome partner, a financial break through that you learn about

or big new tax benefits that are available for
the asking.

<u>Lesson</u> <u>Learned</u> #6 – Only invite a new partner into your business when it's an absolute necessity or there's an extraordinary reason to enhance your business future. There's much less risk to hire employees that can be terminated for "cause" or necessity.

Be aware that all business mergers are full of risks and challenge but never say never. Signing your name to <u>personally</u> <u>guarantee</u> anything is equally dangerous to the success of your future, peace of mind, and your family security.

NO partners, NO mergers, should never be "cast in stone" when you're making business decisions. Consider all possibilities before jumping to a decision. Change happens and there are valuable reasons on both sides of the question that can be good for you as well as your employees and the business.

Some investors focus on business mergers as well as bringing in new partners or new employees with specialized expertise with the ability to change the success level of your firm, thereby increasing your net worth.

Some decisions may cut across your comfort level, borrowing or taking on risks that can push you into an uncomfortable position of worry and concern.

There are few risks that override the personal guarantee demands of your banker or sometimes a vendor. Professional advice is non-negotiable, you must have it from the best expert legal counsel available.

Good intentions are awesome but there are good reasons NOT to accept unnecessary obligations. Understanding the reasons for incorporating your business is mandatory.

As you probably know, most firms regularly issue credit terms to their clients/customers in good faith that payment will be forth coming according their terms.

Everyone enjoys the convenience of payment scheduling, discounts, too. However, let's assume a market glitch in your business, change happens, your cash flow and credit terms are suddenly devastated.

Sidebar: Our business dropped off 40% in sales the year that we purchased a brand new and very expensive computer system for our small firm. Surprise? Absolutely! Survival became the obvious challenge.

Our computer system vendor took a huge hit on his business, too. As I recall, he suffered a 50 to 60% drop in sales at the same time.

Six (6) months passed before we were able to pay ONE thin dime toward our new computer system debt. Every month, Murray (the owner) told us "Don't worry about it"... words that you should never expect to hear from a vendor in the lifetime.

At the time, interest rates were 20%+ to borrow money from the local bank IF you could even get a loan.

Then and NOW… we call it a GOD thing when our business got carried over this huge debt "hump" with kindness from our vendor.

After 6 months, and NOT one dime of interest charged by the vendor, our bank loaned us the funds to pay in full for the new computer system.

Most big firms have legal counsel on staff or retainer to secure and protect their company assets. Unfortunately, small firms are more often unprepared and lack the needed expertise to see the "bullet" coming.

Many small business owners are easily persuaded (suckered) into signing a personal guarantee when requested by a vendor's legal counsel, just a good faith thing to do.

Sidebar: Banks were paying 1 or 2% annual interest on deposits while loans were at 5 or 6% interest. Vendors continued to add 18% interest terms which was license to steal money from their customers for late payments.

You need to know and understand what can happen when a vendor's legal counsel gets involved and throws you a massive curve ball. Obviously, business lawyers are well trained, well-practiced, in "legalese" while most of us have no clue.

Reality is that your invoices originally came to your LLC or 3rd party corporate structure unless you're a proprietor of the business. My guess is that your legal counsel set up your personal liability protection on DAY ONE when you first set up your business.

Never, never, never break your protection of the 3rd party business license just to be Mr. Nice guy to your vendors. It's wrong for them to even ASK for a personal guarantee.

Your business takes a nose dive (like ours did) and you get a very nice and courteous letter from your vendors' legal counsel asking for the owners of your firm (maybe YOU) to sign a personal guarantee (just in case), "your company runs out of money" or files for bankruptcy.

First, don't do it! Next, confer with your own legal counsel to make sure you make the right decision. IF you do sign the agreement, your 3rd party protections just left the premises.

As of the day you sign a personal guarantee, not only are your company assets on the line, your <u>personal</u> <u>assets</u> are now pledged to underwrite (guarantee) your entire corporate debt, not a wise move for any of us.

If you're like most of us, with competitors coming out your ears, vendors working on your weakest emotions and suggesting you lock yourself into a lifetime of corporate liability, it's little wonder that you'd like to stay in bed rather than go to work where the phone is ringing off the hook with threats and ugliness you've never known.

An old saying is.... "Nice guys (gals) finish last" but we believe otherwise. There are fair and equitable ways and means to running your business that will pay dividends long-term.

Living your life in a state of gratitude with a thankful heart is where all your blessings will continue to flow in and out of your business.

Always believe that good is coming, keep the faith under all circumstances, and work hard and simply do your best, good "karma" is on its way.

Sidebar: Maybe we should follow this guy. He lost everything but went to a friend and asked to borrow enough money to buy a new Lexus to drive so he'd have the appearance of success. Not my style but it may work for his business and especially impress his clientele.

Lesson Learned #7 – Join the best industry groups that you can find locally, actually, anywhere. Even better would be a group that only allows one firm in your local area so there are no competitors.

Also, your particular industry may have its own group that allows one firm from your city or state where sharing is open between each member and some member firms actually conduct audits on any of its members who request it to learn best practices in the industry.

In our largest industry we belonged to a national group made up of firms from different cities across the USA. There was a basic level of service required but it was very reasonable. You didn't have to be in the top tier of competitors to be invited to become a member.

Some of us audited several members at NO cost which turned out to be our most valued benefit. Yes, travel and hotel expenses were covered by the firm being audited but that cost was maybe 10% of the value.

Being in a peer group was extremely valuable to each member. Everyone was willing to share financial statements, operating reports and other information when requested by member firms.

Trust in the group was exceptional and respect was at the highest level. However, there was a requirement that if you sell your business to a national player then its good bye forever. It was understood that this would happen to our best members when the value of their business drew the attention of big competitors. Don't recall any problems at all when we sold our business.

Even after we sold our business to a National firm we remained friends with those in the association. Total Trust had been solidly established with the members without question, fear or concern.

Lesson Learned #8 – be a speaker whenever possible for your business or industry. Become known as the spokesperson that people, especially journalists, turn to when they have questions or want a story about your industry. Join up with reputable groups, take advantage of leadership opportunities.

Yes, I know that SPEAKING before a group of people is said to be more feared than death by most of us. However, it doesn't have to be that way for you at all. IF you are fearful of speaking then join the local Speakers Institute for a 3 day training course, if available.

Toastmasters is an open forum in most cities where members follow a leadership team of expert speakers. There's a nominal cost to join where you'll be immediately exposed to excellence as a public speaker. Your fears of speaking will subside as you begin to participate in the club activities where speaking is a regular occurrence for every member.

Speaking to groups in your town or city can do wonders for your easy connection to the top executives in many luncheon or evening clubs where speakers in are demand. The more you do it the easier it will become to stand in front of any group to share your wisdom.

You'll be pleasantly surprised and very pleased at what speaking to various groups will do for your self-esteem as well as your business.

Lots of weekly meetings need speakers. Some groups are small and have 10, 25, maybe 50 members and others may have 100 plus. Your goal is to get industry exposure and share valuable information with the members in each group who are primarily business executives.

Rotary, Kiwanis are just two (2) groups that have weekly speakers, the LIONS Club is another charitable group where speakers are invited on a regular basis for meetings.

Maybe your women's or men's groups at church will be interested in what you have to say. "Ask and ye shall receive" works for many speakers seeking an audience.

Lesson Learned #9 – Build your business with ONE goal in mind. A time will come when your business is recognized as extremely valuable and someone will want to BUY it from you.

Size is not important at this juncture. It might be a local competitor or a big regional player that gets interested in adding your business to their own in your city. Be open to listening, accept a few offers to evaluate. It's worth doing, I assure you, as well as fun and an ego booster.

It's possible that your success will make you a buyer of other services rather than being bought but time changes things, your desire to buy or sell will change. Nothing stands still forever. Normally the buyers today become the sellers of tomorrow.

We sold our business to a National player and cashed out of the business about the time we'd normally retire. However, it's more about timing and industry changes that are happening where you are.

Business buyers are sometimes "cagy" and secretive while others are totally open and serious, you'll know when they are ready to move, to roll out the big bucks, offering excellent payouts for your business.

All you want is to be at the right place, at the right time. Obviously, nobody wants to buy a loser or non-profit service. However, you will never know a buyers true motivation. It may be your location but more likely your high performance staff and good clientele.

Never accept your first offer is the usual advice in the marketplace. Personally, I would never say never, because someone may be willing to pay a high premium for (it doesn't matter!) your business.

Sure, it (could be) your reputation, your staff, your location or even something totally "off the wall" as far as you are concerned.

If you think about it, who cares, as long as you feel good about the reputation of the buyer, the fair treatment of your staff, the money feels "right" and you're ready to cash out.

Usually, there's another buyer or two ready to do a quick and cheap deal if you have to sell out at the wrong time, especially when the marketplace takes a nose dive, interest rates are out the roof, or the competition is brutal.

You can watch the "buyers" system work at a car auction. An Auctioneer is moving around from buyer to buyer, some wave a flag, others move their little finger, twist their nose, wink, and another smiles and looks around waiting for the next move.

The first offer may be $5K and the end buyer pays $100K for the very same restored car. What happened? The auctioneer has just sorted out the various reasons and values known only to the players who keep moving the price UP until the real buyer lays down the cash.

Lesson Learned #10 – Guarantee all services for your customers or you'll lose many who are not risk takers. Why should anyone other than yourself or your company provide assurances of value? Everyone is entitled to their money back if your product or service fails.

One of the challenges in today's marketplace are Internet Marketers who expect payment before you get the product. Unfortunately, some business owners are not truthful or honest, very unfortunate for the honest business executive with total integrity.

Well known IM names have sold "do it for you" promises and scammed buyers out of thousands of dollars then reneged on the follow-through with the customer. It happens, be aware.

All of us know the phrase "NO GUARANTEE" or NO WARRANTY" on a car windshield which tells us the seller assumes no responsibility if the car falls apart when you drive it off the lot. Personally, I would never assume the liability or warranty on the vehicle.

New car warranties are suspect when you read the "fine" print and see the word "limited" or take at your own risk. OK, maybe they're too smart to put in a "direct" risk but reading the "fine" print is worth your time and protection, otherwise it's your risk to assume.

Buying a new house, a vacation timeshare, maybe a boat falls into the same category of "let the buyer beware" or you get 3 days to change your mind in some states. Otherwise, you're stuck with the mortgage forever with no escape hatch anywhere and the builder has a big negative mark when you check with the BBB (Better Business Bureau).

Lesson Learned #11 – Never put yourself at personal risk. It sounds better than it is when new risks, trials and tribulations come down the pike every day in the world of running a business.

Maybe we should add "except" because never is a big challenge when you're dealing with contractors, new agreements, large vendors, business partners, vendors, salesmen/women and the list never ends.

There is RISK in life, in business, at rest or simply sitting in your easy chair having a cool brew before bedtime.

Guess we could say this lesson is "tongue in cheek" because it falls into the impossible category. However, the lesson remains because it alerts us to the necessity of seeking the wisdom of our advisors rather than thinking it's no big deal or we can handle it on our own.

<u>Lesson</u> <u>Learned</u> #12 – Be sure all licenses, certificates, inspections are done according to the law and documented. Even those you don't agree with or you feel there's NO legitimate reasons for such a rule to be applied to your business. Do it anyway!

Few business owners enjoy paying fees that are levied by the local licensing office, the register of deeds, project inspectors who never smile or give an inch, or whomever is in charge of sending tax notices.

Just understand that your rants and road rage is falling on deaf ears, no one is listening. Clerks don't care so give them your check for fees, a big smile and move on to building your business.

Until you can connect with the inspectors or find a legitimate out you may as well not fight the system. Your government needs money to support their greedy habits whether you agree with them or not.

There's always somebody who wants to stir up trouble or fight some issue that's cast in concrete for the next century. IF business success and growth is your goal then spend your energy and time working on new plans, new opportunities that will take you to the next level.

Lesson Learned #13 - build your business with integrity and outshine the competition. Become the "go to" person in your industry where everyone knows they can get an honest answer without fluff. Peter built his house on the ROCK and you can build your business with a solid foundation too.

The biggest competitor to your business is usually in your own place of business. Worrying about outsiders or supposed competition is a total waste of your time and energy. Get over it! Focus on your customers and services provided, your employees, your follow up systems and your business goals. There will be NO time to worry about any of your competitors in the marketplace.

Rather than more Lessons Learned, we'll call the following #14 and #15 which will contain more wisdom and value than all the others put together.

Are you agreeable? Fair enough! Once I get on a roll, look out, we've only hit the high road so far and the real value is still to come.

Diversion is sometimes a good thing. Takes your mind off the now to focus back yonder where it all took place or as I remember it.

You may not agree with some of the 13 Lessons Learned but each one comes from personal experience as an entrepreneur. Some come from family history of lessons learned in earlier years that stuck in my mind as "watch out" alerts in the business arena.

Some ideas surfaced because someone in the family got scammed or cut out of their earned income or position, even business ownerships that were promised but never were sealed with documentation.

First, I think of my Dad, a great guy, lived the good life, served his church as Treasurer for over 25 years, worked 43 years in the warehousing business for a "gentleman" named Mr. Smith who was a "playboy" in his day but mostly a big risk taker.

Dad owned 8% of the business but I have no recall or knowledge of how that came about. Maybe it was a gesture of kindness by Mr. Smith or it may have been a "Slick Willie" to secure loyalty from his top Executive.

Let's "assume" it was from his good heart, not selfishness, to help us give the story a more refreshing and uplifting appearance for us.

Anyhow, here's the bigger problem. Mr. Smith told Dad that his future was secure when death or retirement came to the (much older) owner, Mr. Smith, he would <u>make</u> <u>sure</u> that the business "WOULD" become..... You guessed it! Mr. Smith died but had NEVER put pen to the promise so it DID NOT happen. An unfortunate experience that you don't want to happen in your future as an executive working for a business owner or anywhere that you have earned or been promised a big gift that never arrives.

Mr. Smith had two adult children who had never been in the business but by WILL they inherited the business (92%) as usually happens, it's the American way to leave your assets to your children.

Don't let it happen to YOU! It's imperative that anything, everything you are promised, told by your boss or even "suggested" requires LEGAL documentation. Otherwise, "IT" will NOT become yours in the future.

Conversations or commitments are just that, some of us call it nothing but "blowing smoke". Intention has NO value until it has been legalized and documented according to the law.

Being a nice person, we can even say that Mr. Smith was a good fellow and his intentions were probably made in good faith. It was simply very unfortunate that time or circumstance, maybe convenience of the day never allowed for the necessary time to "get 'er done".

However, it cost the remaining employee, with 43 years of loyalty, to be left without the 92% of the business stock ownership that was or seemed to be promised to him. Not a good day! Agreed?

Suddenly, I had a flash recall working in the warehouse business for a short time in my teen years and a Mr. Mann came to mind. As a teenager, it was his big new Lincoln Town Car that impressed us. Mr. Mann was a traveling salesman and did extremely well according to the latest gossip around the office.

Dad did a lot of extra work for Mr. "M" and was promised $3K in the old man's WILL (more like $50K today). It never happened as you probably guessed, same simple legalese oversight but we remember Mr. Mann fondly.

Sidebar: There's a thrill to writing about these experiences because this knowledge from the past turned into millions of dollars for some of us who were "listening".

LOTS MORE TO COME....

Some of these issues (remembrances) come from my recall of the past while other times are from my own personal experiences. These are not things that only happened to us, it's universal, and the majority are everyday occurrences in the world of business and life.

Perfect families, a perfect business, or the perfect life are only available on the other side of the "pearly gates" where Jesus reigns.

As long as we're on this side of life there will be challenges for each of us to seek answers that are fair and good for all, especially those that are in your control, mine, too.

Lots of challenges and opportunities surface between brothers, sisters, cousins, siblings everywhere. Maybe you've seen it between

Uncles and In-laws doing business with each other. Some issues are the kind that can turn families into bitter enemies or great friends.

Many, probably most, of our problems come from misunderstandings or knowing just enough to have NO clue about the real situation.

Family members do things that we don't understand, what's the reason or purpose, who's pushing the issue? I'll give you an example below in my own family.

These are the kind of stories that I love. Charlie is a family member, one of the brothers that left the farm for the big city, and Roy is an in-law married to a sister. Nice guy, knows everybody, delivers the mail every day through dirty and dusty roads, rain or shine, makes no difference, the mail has to go, so says the postal service, right?

Anyhow, in the early days an acre of land was fairly cheap to buy. The family was not rich or poor either but grandpa had 500 acres of land that he left to his 8 children. Obviously, there was the old home place that turned into a problem between the in-laws and siblings.

Ralph, another in-law had his eye on getting the home place because.... (I never did figure this one out) but he never got it which makes the most sense.

As you might expect, this created a problem in getting the estate divided and caused the eldest brother, the appointed administrator, a nightmare in the process.

The home place was shared by his two youngest sisters who were school teachers and lived at the home place during the summer months on vacation but lived in the teacher's quarters in other cities during the wintertime.

Simple solution.... Do nothing for the next 25 years and a few die along the way to make it easier to settle the estate. Anyway, Ralph was the cause of the problem and ended up being the loser too.

Almost forgot Charlie's problem. He needed money and his 50 acres turned into his bargaining chip. Actually, he moved to another town and was no longer around the farm property. Roy was the in-law and he liked to "make a buck" whenever the opportunity showed up.

Here's the problem as I see it, the unknown pieces of the puzzle. Two tales were passed along but nothing was written down. Questions turn into a family debate even though there are no answers.

The BIG question! Did Charlie really need money or did Roy talk a little bit of "poor mouth" persuading him to sell his inherited 50 acres?

A bigger question surfaces between siblings because it was known that Roy was a very shrewd trader, negotiator and land buyer.

Land with <u>big</u> <u>timbers</u> was very valuable. Speculation was that Charlie had no clue about his land value and got scammed in the details. Did he? Don't really know, for sure, but some say he got a raw deal from Roy, the in-law but I'm guessing he out smarted him.

Is there a valuable message in the details? Absolutely, however, not in the details that surfaced between Charlie and Roy. It's all behind the scenes that brings out the smart actions necessary for everyone.

Remember, even if you have an experience or reason to dislike lawyers they are sometimes necessary. IF you are negotiating, trading, selling, buying anything or setting up a business partnership or ownership you need legal counsel, your own, always.

Like Charlie, selling his 50 acres, he should have sought the knowledge of a forester and legal counsel rather than simply accepting Roy's offer. Most of us think the "handshake" is good enough and maybe it should be but seldom is that the best way to build goodwill for all, especially you.

Nothing is better than a win/win for everyone regardless whether it's buying houses, raw land, negotiating contracts, getting married or divorced, it's always "better safe than sorry" (an old saying!).

Have you ever gone into another room and forgot the "why"? Just a simple example of why all of us need to "write" down our agreements with each other, family members, friends, job applicants, employers, etc.

You've heard someone say, "That's NOT what I said" or "I didn't say that" or something similar but without a written document. None of us can be sure what was said in tone or verbiage. He promised me a raise in 90 days, benefits, insurance, a car, etc. Did he, really?

You'll have an opportunity to invest in the new restaurants that we're building and earn more money as a partner in this business. Sound good? Maybe, maybe not, right? Who knows, NOT you. Make sure you separate out what you are negotiating at the time, not "pie in the sky" or another "just talking" bit or "blowing smoke" again.

What do you see when you look back into your past? Hopefully it's not eleven (11) years in prison; three (3) marriage failures or even worse for some but it's said that everyone has a story to tell the rest of us.

HAVE YOU ENCOUNTERED EMINENT DOMAIN?

Did the local power company come across your farm land, like it did ours, pay a few bucks and destroy millions of dollars in value. Rather than 46 acres in pristine condition we have four (4) huge big foot line holders (power lines) covering fourteen (14) acres with negative restrictions and non-negotiable limits. Just the simple realities of life that some of us have learned to accept as fair for the good of all.

At this stage of life, long past 3 score and 10, it's not worth being bitter about anything that has the potential to destroy your happiness. Just the other day, I heard Joel Osteen say..."all is well" regardless of what's happening in your life or business, makes sense to me.

I'm reminded of the story told about the lady who died and had requested a "spoon" in her hand because she had always heard that the best was yet to be. Fortunately, I believe that's true and hope you do, too!

As I mentioned before, my Dad was really a good man in his small world and he did some good things that protected us from harm or danger. We ate well, dressed well, lived like absolute Kings compared to many who grew up in our middle class neighborhood.

My Mom was awesome too. She had ONE sister and seven brothers which explains why

I only have ONE brother. I'm guessing she spent her early life changing lots of diapers and was very happy to leave the family farm at an early age for the big city.

In fairness to my Dad's family, it's only in good faith that Mom's family should get equal time. Actually, between both farms there's almost 800 acres to negotiate. Maybe Duke Power (no intention!) actually evened the score between the family farms even though 20 miles apart in different counties.

It's hard to believe what happened after Mom left her family farm but it actually involves the same power company under the power of "eminent Domain" again.

Sidebar: Recall that "eminent Domain" takes your property for the good of the community "supposedly" at a *"fair" price.*

As you know, WATER is critical to the power company, right?

My grandmother, bless her soul, owned 300 acres of land that was "suddenly" <u>surrounded</u> by a huge lake formed from the newly built dam called <u>Lake Norman</u>. Mom's youngest brother never worked another day in his life, drove new Cadillac's every year and became the "gentleman" farmer.

I don't have to tell you that the <u>land values skyrocketed</u> and a bunch of good ole' country boys got rich. It does seem that every story has a glitch, right?

It's another one of those stories where he said, she said, but there's never any proof (at least none found by us!) covering a few past agreements except the one that really counts and got "legally" <u>written down</u>.

You heard about the youngest brother and his new Cadillac every year and whatever else he wanted was NO problem. He and his bride never had any kids but they did stick around and take care of Grandma until she passed. Some of us wondered where new cars were located for the rest of the siblings, me too.

One brother seemed more educated than the others because he served as a County Agent or something to do with helping the local farmers. My recall is that he "stumped" his big toe at forty (40) and ended up getting married and had a couple of daughters.

My gut says he probably had a hand in doing the right thing, he was a good guy. However, the words "FEE SIMPLE" were written on an agreement that turned everything upside down for all but ONE smart cousin.

The youngest brother never left home but got married and brought his young bride into the home to share all the benefits of NO house payments, over 200+ FREE acres to farm or whatever he chose to do.

Ironically, he soon learned about Government payments or subsidies that the farmers were getting for NOT planting tobacco, cotton, etc. so he got free cash, too.

That's not everything! He "talked" his sisters and brothers into signing off to give him a life estate ownership in the farmland so the bank would loan him the money needed to remodel the old farmhouse.

After some hesitation, all the siblings agreed to sign over their ownership in the farm property with the understanding that it would eventually return to them or at least as an inheritance to their children.

What do you think? Sounds like a fair plan to me. Supposedly, the agreement was signed and gave lifetime estate ownership that would allow the rebuilding or remodeling of the old farm house.

After living with an outhouse (toilet) beside the old granary or meat house, for the record, it was a two holler, the upscale model, but not exactly the desirable situation for his bride as well as his Mom.

Anyhow, not exactly what everyone wanted but it was only a lifetime ownership transfer according to the farm agent brother.

Sidebar: In fairness to all, I'm thinking that he "assumed" that his youngest brother would do the right thing or die without a WILL which would, by state law, return the farmland to the grandchildren because he had none of his own..

The rude awakening came when the youngest brother "kicked the bucket" at (91), all the sisters and brothers were deceased and the grandchildren got a huge surprise in their inheritance letter except for ONE of them.

Unfortunately, there's always a "kiss butt" smart one that knows the rules and gets up

close where everything gets changed for her
benefit.

Gerry-Dean
worked for a large philanthropy firm, you'd
recognize the name, we'll let it remain
anonymous, but she got a super kind of
education in how charities work, how "stuff"
should be managed to be sure it goes where
you want it. She discovered that the farmland,
the estate, was given <u>fee</u> <u>simple</u> to the
youngest brother rather than a life estate
which changed everything.

 Watch this! Suddenly, we noticed that she had moved into a new "double wide" with her new husband right beside the old farmhouse where the Uncle still lived.

Now, it's time to go to work on setting up the plan for her future inheritance, cutting out all the other grandchildren except for a few crumbs they should receive after Uncle died.

Another surprise was…. had Gerry-Dean died before her latest husband, HE would have inherited the estate but he smoked himself to death and she ended up as the lucky winner of about 90% of the estate value.

One lucky grandkid got $158K because he visited Uncle on occasion and took them KFC for dinner. A couple got $74K while the rest got $27K or as little as $13K for some reason but it was wrong and bad Karma on her part to change the Will or intent for her benefit.

IF you got this far, the story turned into a soap opera, but still I hope you see the big picture of how easily things can turn upside down when important estate planning gets handled by amateurs or family members who "assume" everything is correctly handled until the reading of the WILL.

One huge glitch in the "new" Will specified that everything had to be sold at the time of death which meant economic values in the real estate market was a non-issue.

As you know, values go up and down and caught Gerry-Dean in a down market which meant she got several million less because of the unfortunate timing of Uncle's death.

None of us can beat God's system. Live by His rules and even if or when bad happens there is a silver lining for you in the end.

CONCLUSION

Everyone enjoys the possibility of receiving an inheritance from their parents, Uncles, Aunts, siblings, even a special friend.

None of us want to discover that someone has taken advantage of a situation which cuts us out of our entitlements or inheritance.

I wrote this book to bring your attention and awareness to how it can happen right under your nose without a clue.

Understanding FEE SIMPLE is critical knowledge for your benefit. Don't count on anyone other than your own legal counsel for advice.

Realize that "talk" is NOT the same as total commitment or intention on your behalf.

Don't be shy! When anyone says "I'm going to leave you my?? Then ASK…. Is that written down in your WILL? Otherwise, don't count on it.

Your OWN WILL is probably the most important document you should have today yet it's often reported that only about 30% of us even have a WILL. IF that's you then let us encourage you to move with haste to get it done today or as soon as you possibly can in the near future.

About the Publisher

Don Monteith is the owner of DRM Publishing and spent 32 years in the Staffing business before he began sharing his entrepreneurial experiences for the Small business Owners of America. He lives in NC with his bride, has 3 grown children, 7 grand's to make life a joy and blessing. Don enjoys sharing his experiences in hopes that learning in the SHK (School of Hard Knocks) can be missed by many who read his writings about business and how to enjoy the fullness of life.

We invite YOU to join us on the sites below along with other readers of our Kindle books so everyone can share their comments and thoughts with each other.

https://www.facebook.com/groups/donmonteith

www.Facebook.com/actiontips

Twitter.com/DonMonteith

ONE LAST THING.

If you enjoyed this book or found it useful I'd be very grateful if you'd post a short review on Amazon. Your support really does make a difference and I read all the reviews personally so I can get your feedback and make this book even better.

If you'd like to leave a review then all you need to do is click the review link on this book's page on Amazon here:

Thanks again for your support!

www.ingramcontent.com/pod-product-compliance
Lightning Source LLC
Chambersburg PA
CBHW070843180526
45168CB00002B/937